CALLAHAN LIBRARY
ST. JOSEPH'S COLLEGE
25 Audubon Avenue
Patchogue, NY 11772-2399

Reflective Supervision in Practice:

Stories from the Field

by Rebecca Parlakian, Editor
ZERO TO THREE
Washington, D.C.

i

ACKNOWLEDGMENTS

We gratefully acknowledge The David and Lucile Packard Foundation, whose leadership support has launched the Center for Program Excellence and its publications. We also extend our thanks to the William Randolph Hearst Foundation and the W. Clement and Jessie V. Stone Foundation for their generous support of the Center's work.

We extend special thanks to the staff members and professionals who helped to shape, write and edit and this publication, including:

ZERO TO THREE Reviewers:

Monimalika Day, Ph.D.
Linda Eggbeer, M.Ed.
Emily Fenichel, M.S.W.
Andrea Grimaldi, M.S. Ed.
Nancy Guadagno
Nancy L. Seibel, M.Ed., NCC
Joan Melner, M.S.

Expert Reviewers:

Linda Gilkerson, Ph.D., Erikson Institute
Alicia F. Lieberman, Ph.D., San Francisco General Hospital
Trudi Norman-Murch, Ph.D., CCC-SLP, Southwest Human Development
Candice Percansky, M.A., Erikson Institute and Ounce of Prevention Fund
Karen Wollenburg, M.S., The Portage Project

An Additional Resource for Infant/Family Programs:

To access an Internet-only supplement to this publication — titled **"The Ounce of Prevention Fund: A Case Study in Implementing Reflective Supervision"** — visit the ZERO TO THREE Center for Program Excellence Web site at www.zerotothree.org/cpe.

ZERO TO THREE

Suite 200
2000 M Street, NW
Washington, DC 20036-3307

www.zerotothree.org

Copyright © 2002 by ZERO TO THREE.
All rights reserved.

ISBN 0-943657-59-8

Suggested citation:
Parlakian, R (Ed.). (2002). *Reflective supervision in practice: Stories from the field.* Washington, DC: ZERO TO THREE.

Additional copies of this monograph are available from ZERO TO THREE. Call (800) 899 4301 or visit our Web site at http://www.zerotothree.org/.

INTRODUCTION

All program leaders share the same high expectations for their organizations: to provide quality services to families, to encourage effective staff-family relationships, and to see high levels of enthusiasm and low levels of turnover among their staff. The following case studies feature organizations that have chosen to use reflective supervision as one tool to support the achievement of these goals. Reflective supervision is the practice of meeting regularly with staff members to discuss their experiences, thoughts, and feelings related to the work. The role of the supervisor is to help the supervisee answer his or her own questions by

- providing support and knowledge to guide decision making;
- offering empathy to help supervisees explore their own reactions to the work; and
- helping staff members manage the stress and intensity of work with families.

Supportive relationships between staff members and leaders are the foundation for nurturing relationships between parents and children. Strong supervisory relationships provide the staff with a model of, and experience with, supportive, individualized responses. With families as with staff members, this approach encourages learning and growth, as well as mutuality and collaboration. It creates a supportive framework that assists parents in providing their children with the nurturing care they need to thrive. At every level of the program—for supervisors, the staff, and families—reflective supervision plays a crucial role in encouraging positive outcomes through mutual respect, partnership, and open communication.

This publication highlights four infant-family programs that chose to implement reflective supervision. Each profile, co-authored by and based on interviews with program staff members, discusses the impetus for change, the key elements of the transition, and the outcomes the program experienced as a result of using reflective supervision. After each profile, program leaders will find several tools designed to help them introduce reflective concepts to their organizations:

- **Questions to Think About,** which can be used for self-reflection or group discussion purposes;
- **Suggested Activities,** which offer readers ideas for how the concepts introduced in case studies may be applied to their particular programs; and
- **How It May Look in Practice,** which provides a sample script for how reflective supervision may look and sound in four different contexts—individual supervision, staff meetings, chance encounters, and check-ins.

For additional ideas on using this material for group training, the appendix, titled *Suggestions for Trainers and Facilitators* (page 26), provides an expanded list of discussion questions.

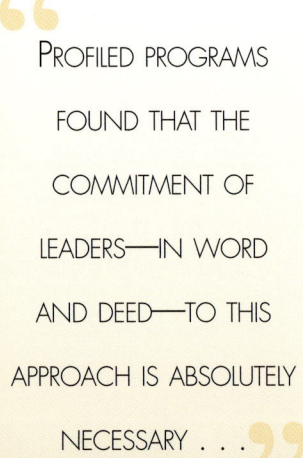

> PROFILED PROGRAMS FOUND THAT THE COMMITMENT OF LEADERS—IN WORD AND DEED—TO THIS APPROACH IS ABSOLUTELY NECESSARY . . .

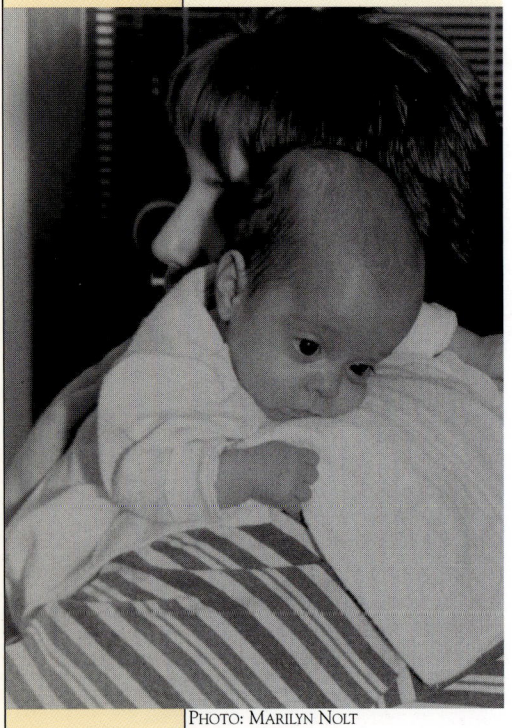

PHOTO: MARILYN NOLT

EXECUTIVE SUMMARY

Reflective supervision is sometimes viewed as difficult to implement in the "real world." Many program leaders and staff members feel too pressured to consider having regular supervisory meetings. Each of the following programs grappled with this and other challenges. Each program resolved these issues differently. The result is a cross-section of experiences, highlighting the roles of and organizational culture, staff needs, and program objectives in implementing reflective supervision.

Several important commonalities exist across profiled programs:

- Implementing reflective supervision was a process—one that, in most cases, took longer than expected. Typically, the transition consisted of a series of incremental changes as each supervisor and staff member made small modifications in practice and personal style over a period of several years.
- Staff members *and* supervisors received supervision on a regular basis. The inclusion of supervisors was crucial because the experience of receiving reflective supervision helped them better understand its practice and feel more comfortable providing it to their staff members.
- Reflective supervision was looked upon not as a cure-all, but as one of many tools. Programs discovered that it was the combination of reflective supervision with other opportunities for development and guidance that supported high-quality service, on-going learning, and relationship-based work.
- Program leaders acknowledge that reflective supervision is not easy to maintain. Profiled programs found that the commitment of leaders—in word and deed—to this approach is absolutely necessary if it is to become part of the organization's culture.
- Reflective supervision pays dividends in the quality of services offered to children and families. All profiled programs experienced positive programmatic outcomes—across-the-board increased staff effectiveness—as a result of utilizing reflective supervision.

WHAT DO YOU MEAN WHEN YOU SAY...?

To guide readers through the following profiles, pertinent vocabulary is defined below. Although these terms have other definitions, they are thought of in this publication and at ZERO TO THREE in the following ways (Parlakian, 2001a):

- **Reflective Supervision**—Supervision that is focused on learning from work with families, that is supportive and collaborative in nature, and that occurs on a reliable schedule. It is characterized by active listening and thoughtful questioning by both supervisor and supervisee. Reflective supervision can take various forms, for example, individual supervision, group supervision, or peer supervision.
- **Reflection**—Stepping back from the moment. Reflection is an opportunity to wonder about, explore, and brainstorm possible responses to work-related challenges. It is a key component of reflective supervision.
- **Collaboration**—Sharing responsibility and control of power within the program. Collaboration is a key component of reflective supervision.
- **Regularity**—Ensuring that supervision takes place regularly with sufficient time allocated to its practice. The frequency of meetings may vary depending on the format of supervision (e.g., group or individual) and the individual staff member's needs.
- **Parallel process**—The way in which positive supervisor-staff relationships set a strong foundation for positive staff-family relationships and vice versa.
- **Relationship-based work**—An approach to work in which quality relationships, characterized by trust, support, and growth, exist among leaders, staff, parents, and children. Relationships are valued, not as a touchy-feely nicety, but as a foundation for providing high-quality service and are supported at all levels of the program.

OREGON EARLY HEAD START

by Rebecca Parlakian and Talley Dunn
Oregon Early Head Start Interviewees:
Talley Dunn, Program Coordinator
Lauren Bell, Site Supervisor
Laura Bellah, Family Specialist

Southern Oregon Early Head Start Program

Where: Central Point, Oregon
Mission: To provide opportunities for children and parents to achieve success with dignity
Target population: Children ages birth to 5 years who have a disability or who are from a low-income family and their families
Program Model: National child development program with center- and home-based components
Introduced Reflective Supervision: 1995
Catalyst for Change: The goal as a start-up program to implement best practices
Frequency of Supervision: Individual supervision provided twice per month to supervisors and direct-service staff

Background on Southern Oregon Early Head Start

In 1994, the federal Early Head Start (EHS) program was created by the U.S. Congress as part of the reauthorization of the Head Start Act. Oregon's two EHS sites were among the first programs established. EHS is a comprehensive child development program with both center-based and home-based components. Its primary objectives are the promotion of healthy parent-child relationships and the delivery of other individualized services, including education and early childhood development, medical, dental, mental health, and nutrition services.

The program philosophy of Oregon Early Head Start (OEHS) is that healthy development is best promoted within the context of nurturing relationships with a primary caregiver who is responsive to children's individual needs. Parents, as the primary educators of their children, are included as full partners in all OEHS services.

THINKING ABOUT REFLECTION

Talley Dunn, program coordinator, notes, "Being [in the first wave of EHS programs], we were really seeking the best possible things to do in setting up our program. I started to get a sense that strong parent-child relationships and sincere relationships between supervisors and staff, and staff and families formed a continuous circle. EHS put a name to it: reflective supervision."

Dunn sought more information about reflective supervision and ultimately decided to integrate elements of reflection and relationship-based work into the OEHS culture. She remembers: "As a manager setting up two centers, the reason we decided to use reflective supervision was to provide high-quality services to infants, toddlers, and their parents. Over time, we've been able to see a parallel—that reflective supervision supports staff, staff support parents, and that parents support their children. It might sound idealistic, but that's what we're hoping for, and that's what we're seeing in our program."

Dunn's mentor, Mary Foltz, an infant-toddler specialist at Portland State University, assisted her with the introduction of reflective supervision. In the planning phases, this mentorship included twice-monthly conference calls to discuss key articles and questions related to reflective supervisory practices. Foltz was then available later in the process to debrief with Dunn after she began providing her staff with supervision.

3

RECRUITMENT, SELECTION, AND STAFF ORIENTATION

As she established the program from the ground up, Dunn sought to hire staff members who were open to the reflective culture she was working to establish at OEHS. Because most job candidates—then and now—have not been familiar with the concept of reflective supervision, Dunn and her team have used specific interview questions to assess job candidates' ability to be reflective about themselves and the work. Examples include the following:

• Do you work best independently or in teams?
• If you had a conflict with your supervisor, what would you do?
• How do you like your supervisor to approach you?

Once on site, new employees meet with their supervisors to learn more about the twice-monthly supervisory meetings for direct-service staff, and to get answers to any specific questions they may have about the process of reflective supervision. Supervisory relationships develop at the staff member's pace and comfort level. "There's no rushing this process," says site supervisor Lauren Bell, who reports to Dunn.

New staff members typically become involved in a supervisory relationship easily because "they see that there's not one way of communicating inside my office and another way outside," says Bell. Through open, supportive interactions with both peers and supervisors, new employees soon realize that reflective supervision is not a specific event but a way of being and communicating throughout the organization. The goal for supervisors is to establish a collaborative relationship with each staff member in which reflective supervision "is as an ongoing dialogue from the day they start until the day they leave," says Bell.

In the early years of the program, Dunn supplemented her targeted recruitment efforts with on-the-job training provided by Victor Bernstein, Ph.D., from the Ounce of Prevention Fund, based in Chicago, Illinois. The purpose of the training was to promote better understanding of reflective approaches among the new staff members at OEHS. Bernstein conducted two full-day training sessions on strengthening the family through strengthening the parent-child relationship. This training, which took place in 1996 and 1997, also addressed observation techniques and the use of videotape to observe family interactions.

MEETINGS CONTRIBUTE TO THE CREATION OF A REFLECTIVE CULTURE

Weekly staff meetings, a group venue to encourage information sharing and collegial support, have become integral to the OEHS program. The value of these regular meetings is two-fold: they encourage collaboration, and they build a sense of commitment to one another and to the work. Each person realizes that, although the work is challenging, he or she is not in it alone.

Bell remembers that her expectations about staff meetings, which were initially focused on administrative tasks and program-centered issues, changed over time: "[I began to] recognize that the need is for us to connect as people, not only as workers." Each meeting now includes a discussion of emerging work-related issues and a time for check-ins during which each staff member updates the others on the previous week. Topics raised may be either professional or personal.

OEHS also uses the following meetings as a way to maximize opportunities for staff collaboration, support, and supervision.

" . . . STAFF MEMBERS NO LONGER FEEL ALONE IN DIFFICULT SITUATIONS "

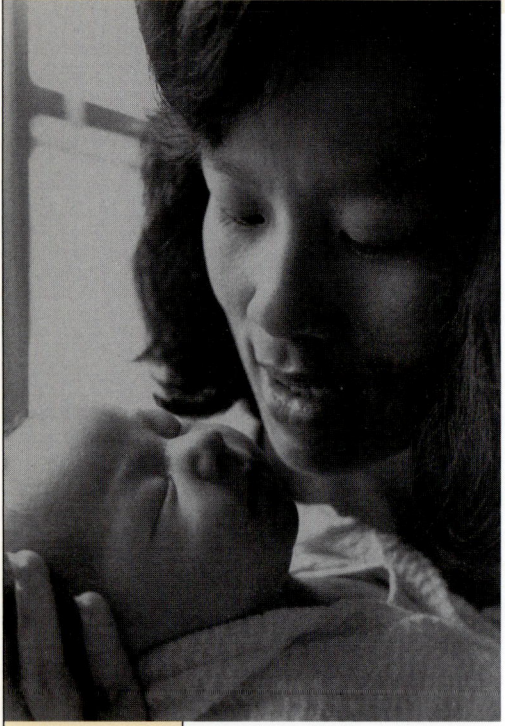

PHOTO: MARILYN NOLT

4

- **Debriefs**—Staff meet after parent-child groups and discuss their immediate observations of interactions, children's growth and development, and the effectiveness of the curriculum plans. Peers listen, support, and encourage one another. Adaptation and revision of curriculum plans takes place at this time.
- **Specialist Support Groups**—Staff members who are working with children and families discuss overall job-related issues and their feelings about the work at these bi-monthly meetings. The specialists, all managing similar caseloads and responsibilities, provide empathy, support, and encouragement to one another.

CHALLENGES TO IMPLEMENTING REFLECTIVE SUPERVISION

Dunn and Bell identify the three most significant challenges they experienced in introducing reflective supervision to the OEHS program. These issues, described below, are not unique to OEHS, but commonly found in many organizations during change management efforts.

Finding the time. Dunn notes that, hands down, the toughest part of using reflective supervision is "always having to make it a priority," as well as knowing when "it's slipping, and then bringing it back to the fore." Says Dunn,

> There are always planning sessions, staff hirings, etc. that supervisory schedules have to accommodate. To [find a balance], supervisors must be convinced of the value of the reflective, collaborative approach, not only for staff but for the well-being of families as well. We need to make it a supervisory priority, creating the time and space for this effort.

Bell agrees, "Reflective supervision is a unique opportunity in the human services field, where outcomes are not always in direct relationship to staff's contribution." She explains that, sometimes, it can be hard for staff members to tell "if they're doing their job well or effectively. The family situation is often an unstable measure. By giving staff an opportunity to discuss their work, they can begin to understand their impact."

Responding to turnover. Turnover, though low at OEHS, is a tremendous challenge for this relationship-based model of supervision. When staff members leave, "you start the relationship anew. You can't rush it. You just need to wait patiently until trust is established," says Dunn.

7 CHARACTERISTICS OF RELATIONSHIP-BASED ORGANIZATIONS

- **Mutuality of shared goals**—often expressed as collaboration and defined in an organizational mission statement
- **Commitment to evolving growth and change**—demonstrated when an organization learns from experience, questions the status quo, and makes changes; ensures that items like mission and vision statements, policies, and procedures accurately reflect the organization's goals, needs, and values
- **Commitment to reflecting on one's work**—institutionalized through the use of supervision that encourages learning from experience
- **Respect for individuals**—promoted through acceptance of individuals for both their strengths and their vulnerabilities; characterized by trust and esteem among colleagues
- **Sensitivity to context**—manifested in the acknowledgment that a particular environment influences the individual within it and vice versa
- **Open communication**—conveyed through a shared belief in the value of others' thoughts, ideas, and feedback
- **Clearly communicated standards for staff**—instituted through widely disseminated, accepted definitions of professional excellence, norms toward which all staff are encouraged to aspire

(Adapted from Bertacchi, 1996)

Learning and applying the concepts. Although Bell agrees that finding the time for reflective supervision is difficult, she does wonder

> "whether time was ever *really* the issue for me since I'm as busy now as I was during start-up. In the beginning, I thought, "There's no way I can do that." During Year 1, there was little time and I was very uncomfortable with [reflective supervision]. I thought I should be all-knowing, like my staff were supposed to come in and for one hour would tell me all their problems and I would give them all the answers. Not surprisingly, I felt some anxiety about "what if I don't have all the answers?" [But] I had misunderstood what reflective supervision was supposed to be.

By meeting regularly with Dunn (her supervisor), Bell grew more comfortable with the concepts of reflective supervision as time went on. "I was looking for a technique, but really reflective supervision was about the relationship between Talley and me. It was Year 3 before I looked forward to supervising staff because I let go of having all the answers. Talley let me experience this in supervision. She would say, 'Tell me about what's happening,' not 'What are all your problems?' I understood how reflective supervision impacted others' work by understanding how it affected me."

In addition, Bell began to see that all her daily interactions with staff were an opportunity to encourage reflective practice. Realizing that "takes the pressure off of something big happening in the one-on-one meetings," she observes. Now, supervisors use groups, lunches, and casual discussions to learn from, share with, and support supervisees. Reflective supervision, says Bell, "is the way in which we have relationships with staff, talk to staff, listen to staff."

Outcomes of Reflective Supervision

One powerful outcome measure tracked by OEHS is its very low turnover—the highest level since 1994 has been only about 12%. This rate compares to an average rate of 30% for the field (Whitebook & Bellm, 1999, p. 5). In addition, the program has achieved a number of important staff development outcomes:

- *Staff members display increased effectiveness in working with families*—for example, watching for subtleties, wondering what families might (or might not) do, finding deeper meaning in their work. Bell notes that, as staff members begin to internalize the concepts of reflection and inquiry, their interactions with families change: "New home visitors are focused on doing, doing, doing." In contrast, she says experienced home visitors "are listening, listening, listening."

- *Staff members better understand how to integrate techniques used in training in their work*—for example, using inquiry and critical thinking skills on the job. By using these techniques to solicit more information about the parents and children with whom they work, staff members can better individualize their responses and interventions to reflect families' needs.

- *Staff members better understand boundary issues*—for example, the need to be more open about and cognizant of how they are affected by families and vice versa. Staff members are better able to use the parallel processes at work in the program to support their own and families' ongoing learning and development.

OEHS has also observed positive outcomes for families as a result of using reflective supervision. Dunn states that parents' problem-solving skills have increased over time because supportive relationships with staff members help them feel more comfortable experimenting with new parenting techniques and approaches.

Finally, Dunn observes that staff members themselves no longer feel alone in difficult situations. "They know that their supervisors will go with them to a home visit or court proceedings. It's letting them know they have a supervisor and colleagues who support them." This level of collaboration ensures that the most difficult questions receive the most comprehensive answers; the most emotionally intense interactions receive the greatest support. OEHS has found that the greatest benefit of reflective supervision lies in the fact that, says Dunn, it "gives everyone an opportunity to step back, observe, and learn from relationships with supervisors, staff, parents, and children."

Questions to Think About

1. Program coordinator Talley Dunn chose to consciously include reflective supervision as an integral piece of the organizational structure she helped create at OEHS. Questions to consider when contemplating this approach include the following:
- How might your organization respond to the introduction of reflective supervision?
- What components of your current organizational structure would support reflective practice?
- What components would make using reflective practice more difficult?

2. Site supervisor Lauren Bell's quote on page 5 is a good example of how "lacking the time to provide supervision" can mask a supervisor's discomfort with the new approach. Questions to consider when thinking about possible obstacles include the following:
- What are the potential obstacles that you might anticipate should you establish regular supervisory meetings with your staff?
- Imagine you have unlimited time, budget capacity, and administrative support. In this environment, what obstacles might prevent you from meeting regularly with staff?
- Compare your two lists. What do the similarities or differences between them tell you?

3. Talley Dunn's vision for how reflective supervision might affect her program was very clear: "The reason we decided to use reflective supervision was to provide high-quality services to infants, toddler, and their families. Reflective supervision supports staff, staff support parents, and parents support their children." Consider the following questions:
- What is your vision for your program?
- How might or might not reflective supervision support this vision?

SUGGESTED ACTIVITY

OEHS uses check-ins during staff meetings. Check-ins are opportunities for each staff member to share with the group an issue that he or she has been thinking about, acting on, or wondering about since the last meeting. These items may be personal or professional in nature—for example, "my daughter is having a really hard time with her math class and she has a big test today" or "I've got great news! The Leggett family just moved into transitional housing."

Today, consider taking a few moments to check-in with others in your group. Or, alternatively, discuss with staff members whether they may want to use check-ins as a way to open staff meetings. Some suggestions for using this approach effectively are listed below.

❶ Outline rules of confidentiality and clarify what types of issues are appropriate to discuss in a group setting.

❷ Establish a structure or format for checking in, including when check-ins occur, approximately how long each individual speaks, etc.

❸ Seek staff support for the change and staff input into the structure of check-ins.

❹ Participate yourself.

❺ Model careful listening skills. (Although the activity does not require that others respond to or comment on check-ins, colleagues must listen attentively.)

❻ Moderate the check-in process, ensuring that the process flows smoothly.

❼ Touch base with staff members after several weeks to see whether checking in is a useful and supportive experience for them.

HOW IT MAY LOOK IN PRACTICE: CHANCE ENCOUNTER IN THE KITCHEN

Program coordinator Talley Dunn and site supervisor Lauren Bell emphasizes the importance of using informal daily interactions—not just scheduled supervision times—as opportunities to promote a reflective approach to work with staff and families. The vignette below provides an example of how an interaction of this kind might look in a child care program.

At 6:00 p.m., Zoe, a new caregiver in the infant room, was sitting in the center's kitchen, holding a cup of coffee and staring off into space with an angry expression. Her supervisor, Gwen, walked in to buy some candy from the vending machine.

G: *Zoe? Are you okay?*

Z: *Sure, I'm fine. [pause] Actually, I just had an argument with a parent.*

G: *[sitting down] What happened?*

Z: *Kate was 45 minutes late picking up Antonio. This the third time this month, and it's always me who has to stay late, since I'm Antonio's caregiver. I mean, I have things to do tonight, you know? And she never calls to let us know she'll be late—just shows up whenever.*

G: *That has to be frustrating.*

Z: *Anyway, finally her car pulls up. She gets out and acts like nothing was wrong. I mean, she was 45 minutes late! But there was no apology. She just said hello and told me she lost track of time at work. Can you imagine? Lost track of time—what about your kid? [pause] And what about me? I mean, I have other things to do besides wait for her.*

G: *Then what happened?*

Z: *Well, I let her know I was pretty annoyed. Then I told her that the last two times she was late, I didn't charge her the late fee, but this time I'd have to. When I explained that it was a dollar a minute, that's when she went ballistic. Said that she'd be complaining to you, and that I had some nerve, and that her work was important and how dare I try to charge her extra after what she's paying for infant care. Then she grabbed Antonio and left.*

G: *Sounds like things didn't end on a happy note for anyone tonight. When you are feeling really angry, it can be hard to have a productive conversation with a parent. I know how it is. I've been in the same situation. It takes a lot of practice to learn to manage those reactions—especially when they might be justified! What are you thinking would be the best thing to do now?*

Z: *Well, I know I still need to talk to her about being late, but the thing is, I'm still angry. I'm just dreading seeing her at drop-off tomorrow morning.*

G: *What do you want to discuss with her?*

Z: *I want to explain that I didn't mean to get angry but that I make plans for the evenings—like tonight I had a ceramics class—and when she's* really late, it puts me in a real bind. It's an issue of respect. I need for her to recognize that I'm a professional, too.

G: *Those are all valid points to raise with Kate. When you see her tomorrow morning, though, I'm wondering what you can do to have a productive conversation?*

Z: *The more I think about it, the more I think that it isn't really about me personally. She's not late to make me angry. She's late because she's late. But somehow I need to make her understand that her being late, whether she realizes it or not, affects me. But I'm afraid that when I try to explain that, I'm going to get mad all over again.*

G: *When I feel myself start to get irritated, sometimes it helps to just wait a second or two before I speak. It gives me some space, I guess—and some time to think about what to say.*

Z: *Sounds like a good idea.*

G: *Can you think of any reasons why Kate is running late so often these days? Until now she's always been on time, I think.*

Z: *I guess it could be something going on at work. She's seemed a little on edge lately. Now that I'm thinking about it, she's mentioned having to work the last few Saturdays.*

G: *That might be something to keep in mind when you're talking with her. You might even want to ask about it.*

Z: *That's a good idea. It'd help to know if she's working on a big project or something. We might be able to modify Antonio's schedule to meet their needs better. And it would just be good to know what's going on.*

G: *That's true. Feel free to stop by before you see her if you want to talk again. And let me know how it goes.*

> " AS A RESULT OF
> REGULAR TRAINING AND
> FEEDBACK SESSIONS WITH
> THEIR PEERS, SUPERVISORS
> BEGAN TO MAKE
> IMPORTANT CHANGES IN
> THE WAY THEY
> SUPERVISED STAFF. "

PHOTO: MARILYN NOLT

by Rebecca Parlakian, Sally Campbell, and Lynn Kosanovich

Healthy Families Alexandria Interviewees:

Sally Campbell, Program Manager

Charlene Giles, Program Supervisor

Lynn Kosanovich, Program Supervisor

Miriam Trigo, Family Resource Specialist

Maria Gonzalez, Family Support Worker

Lourdes Narvaez, Family Support Worker

Healthy Families Alexandria: A Program of Northern Virginia Family Service

Where: Alexandria, Virginia (suburb of Washington, D.C.)

Mission: To strengthen the relationship between vulnerable parents and their children ages birth to 5 years

Target Population: First-time families who are facing multiple challenges (e.g., single parent status, low income, substance abuse problems, victim of abuse or domestic violence, etc.) and who may need additional support at the birth of a child

Program Model: National home visiting initiative designed to improve child health and development and reduce child abuse and neglect

Introduced Reflective Supervision: 1997

Catalyst for Change: Participation in ZERO TO THREE's Cornerstones Project, a quality-improvement initiative for infant-family programs in the Washington metro area

Frequency of Supervision: Direct-service staff—2 hours individual supervision per week; supervisors—2 hours group supervision per week

---

Background on Healthy Families Alexandria

Healthy Families Alexandria (HFA) is one of four Healthy Families programs administered by the Northern Virginia Family Service (NVFS). Established in 1993, the program is affiliated with Healthy Families America, a nationwide initiative designed to promote child health and development as well as to reduce child abuse and neglect.

Using an individualized, family-centered approach, HFA staff members

- ensure that families have a medical provider;
- share information on children's development processes;
- assist families in identifying their baby's needs and in obtaining resources;
- support families in the home while they respond to their children's and their own needs;
- share ideas on caring for infants, toddlers, and young children;
- link families with other resources in the community;
- assist families in following up with recommended immunization schedules; and
- help families to feel more empowered.

IMPLEMENTING REFLECTIVE SUPERVISION

Before introducing reflective practice, Healthy Families programs in the Washington, D.C. area struggled with maintaining a focus on the parent-child relationship in the face of families' multiple challenges. This tension resulted in a working environment in which "home visitors were tired and struggled with burnout, [and] their supervisors were frustrated and feeling inadequate" (Bernstein, Campbell, & Akers, 2001).

Through their participation in Cornerstones—a regional, ZERO TO THREE-based quality-improvement initiative—Healthy Families programs in the Washington metro area hoped to refocus on fami-

ly strengths and parent-child relationships. Intermediary steps to this overall goal included improving infant mental health services to families and providing a more consistent level of training and support to program supervisors by implementing reflective supervision.

As part of this initiative, Healthy Families partnered with Victor Bernstein from the Ounce of Prevention Fund to develop a training and support program for supervisors that introduced the concepts of reflective practice. The program, modeled on the Ounce's *Strengthening Families through Strengthening Relationships* training, focused on how supervisors could encourage staff's efforts to support the parent-child relationship.

In the initial stages of this ongoing training effort, supervisors shared the tension they experienced in balancing staff and families' development within the reality of "too little time, too much to do and too few resources" (Bernstein et al., 2001). Subsequent training sessions with Bernstein encouraged supervisors to identify what was already working in their programs and helped them begin building on their programs' strengths. Experiencing a strengths-based approach themselves supported supervisors as they began to develop strengths-based relationships with staff members. Staff members, in turn, were coached in establishing these relationships with families. This parallel—supervisors learning to build on staff's strengths and staff members learning to build on family strengths—helped to refocus the program on parent-child interaction.

The training also included discussions on how supervisors could shift their attention from case and crisis management and, instead, support staff in their efforts to help parents see their competency with their children. By developing new skills in observation, inquiry, and flexible responses, supervisors began to see their role as one of a mentor or guide, someone who assists staff members as they struggle with—and resolve—challenges related to the work. This new perspective helped to alleviate the pressure of "finding answers" to families' problems, freeing everyone to think more holistically about the family rather than to focus primarily on the family's crises.

Later workshops explored how to gather information rather than make assumptions and how to use questions to help staff members identify possible solutions. This "Inquiry as Intervention" approach—using questions as a way to promote staff and family learning—began to take hold within the organization. Slowly, the group began to understand how to use inquiry productively, learning how to "ask questions that will *help* people," notes Campbell. Lynn Kosanovich, a supervisor who reports to Campbell, adds, "You need to find some middle ground. It's okay to make suggestions to someone. The question is not *whether* to offer suggestions, it's *when* and *how* to do so."

CHANGES TO SUPERVISORY PRACTICES

When staff members from Healthy Families began working with Victor Bernstein, no one could have anticipated how the role of the supervisor would be transformed to support a more family- and child-centered approach to the work. As a result of regular training and feedback sessions with their peers, however, supervisors began to make important changes in the way they supervised staff.

The result was that supervisory sessions evolved into opportunities to think proactively about upcoming home visits and provided opportunities for staff members to explore their feelings about and reactions to the work. Campbell explains the change in supervision: "Instead of advice [which is directive], we offer ideas, suggestions, brainstorming—general options in the problem-solving process. It's a collaborative interaction."

The following anecdote from family resource specialist Miriam Trigo illustrates both the power of reflective supervision and the insight that can be gleaned through parallel processes at work in the program.

> I remember going to visit a family and walking in and saying, "Hello, how's the baby doing?" and talking about the baby the whole time. Then when I went to talk to my supervisor about my families, the first thing she asked was, "Hi, how are you?" and we talked about me as a person for a while. I felt really good, because she cared about *me*. The first thing we talked about wasn't how many assessments I had done, or how many families I had visited. And so I learned to go into visits and ask parents, "How

> "THIS PARALLEL—SUPERVISORS LEARNING TO BUILD ON STAFF'S STRENGTHS AND STAFF MEMBERS LEARNING TO BUILD ON FAMILY STRENGTHS—HELPED TO REFOCUS THE PROGRAM ON PARENT-CHILD INTERACTION."

PHOTO: MARILYN NOLT

are you? You were sick the last time I came; are you feeling better now?" It's important that someone cares about *you,* not just your work—and it's the same with families.

In addition to the careful use of questions, supervisors began to use several other strategies during supervisory sessions, including:

- Offering comments, observations, or both (e.g., "I noticed that when you … this happened.")
- Using videotape of home visits to help staff members see themselves and families' interactions more objectively (see section below for a larger discussion on the use of video)
- Gathering information on what staff members have learned or already know about the family

Over time, supervisors began to acknowledge staff members' expert perspective on the families with whom they worked, and staff began to see parents as the experts on their children. Campbell notes that this change marked a big step in the process—one that had a direct effect on services to families. One family support worker remembers: "[Before] when I talked to families I would say, 'Let's do this, let's try this.' Now I say, 'What do you want to do? What have you already tried?' I let them decide and then I support them in that decision."

TOOLS TO SUPPORT REFLECTIVE SUPERVISION

Campbell asserts that "reflective supervision on its own is not enough. Other tools [to support staff-family relationship building] are needed, too." HFA responded by introducing a number of additional resources, including a new curriculum that focused on parent-child interaction. Supervisors also expanded toy lending libraries, helped create traveling toy kits for home visits, and worked with staff members to develop a resource catalog of successful home visiting activities. Family support workers received additional training on early brain development, language development, and videography. They learned how to provide anticipatory guidance to parents on children's development and how to involve parents in routine developmental screenings.

Several tools that proved important to successfully implementing reflective supervision are discussed in the following sections.

SUPERVISION FOR SUPERVISORS

The Healthy Families programs soon realized the importance of providing ongoing support to supervisors as they introduced a reflective approach. As a result, all supervisors began receiving 2 hours of group supervision per week from Campbell. As supervisors experienced reflective supervision themselves, they began to understand the important learning that takes place when individuals step back, observe, and discuss the work. Seeing this dynamic, supervisors were better able to provide their own staff members with optimal learning experiences during supervisory sessions. Looking back, all of the sites in the original Healthy Families project note that providing reflective supervision to supervisors was essential to the success of the initiative.

OBSERVATION AND VIDEOTAPING

"Using video is the most practical way to help staff and families see for themselves what is working now and what might work better in the future," says Campbell. To assist family support workers in focusing on the relationship between parents and children, programs invested in video equipment. Staff began recording parent-child interactions during home visits and found that video allowed them to observe and learn from everyday routines and rituals. Home visitors and parents alike could see how they read one another's and the baby's cues and observe how the baby responded to them.

Parents enjoy the process of filming and viewing as well as the product, which reinforces the centrality of their role in their children's lives. For family support workers, videos give them the concrete information they need to use a strengths-based and reflective approach. In addition, videos helped to highlight staff members' own skills and accomplishments by giving them an opportunity to observe their interactions with families and the effect of their interventions.

Supervisors also began using videos as a tool for learning. They videotaped supervisory sessions and viewed them with their supervisees or with Campbell. Videotaping allows supervisors to see for themselves what worked and what didn't work in their approach with a particular staff member.

RECRUITMENT STRATEGIES

To ensure that new staff (both home visitors and supervisors alike) are a good fit with the reflective model, HFA and other Northern Virginia Family Service's Healthy Families programs changed their job descriptions and employment ads. Campbell notes that the impetus for this shift was the realization by leaders that "most people come into the work wanting to help. What we do is shift their thinking about what help is—giving families the tools they need to do it themselves."

Rather than emphasize "helping families at-risk," job advertisements now highlight the family support worker's role in "supporting families, child development and building skills." Campbell notes, "We try to see if the job candidates can shift their way of thinking. The big question is, Do they assume good intent on the part of the family?" In the interview, candidates respond to questions that ask them to reflect on their personal style and their reactions to common situations encountered on the job.

Supervisory Orientation Program

For new supervisors, HFA instituted a shadowing system in which those new to the role observe experienced supervisors during their training period. When new supervisors have been in the position for a few months, they are observed during a supervisory meeting by a more tenured supervisor or by Campbell. Later, they will discuss with their supervisor what elements of the meeting worked or didn't work. Finally, all supervisors attend a monthly meeting led by Campbell, which is designed to explore the process of supervision and the benefits and challenges of this role. No administrative issues are on the agenda of this meeting.

Challenges to Implementing Reflective Supervision

Because the whole team at HFA went through the transition together, everyone experienced the growing pains that come with learning by doing. Lacking a peer network conversant in these ideas, supervisors and staff alike felt a little "stupid" using reflective supervision initially, says Campbell. She observes: "Looking back, supervisors and staff were remarkably patient." She explains that it's hard to go from feeling really comfortable with your approach "to feeling incompetent while you learn something new."

Staff-supervisor relationships ultimately changed for the better, but the journey was not always easy. Maria Gonzalez, a family support worker, remembers, "In supervision, I always told my supervisor what was going on with my families, and she was always trying to fix it—giving me advice I had already tried. I'd say, 'No, that didn't work, that didn't work.' Finally, she asked me, 'How do you want me to help you?' And I told her I probably just needed her to listen, not to give me advice." The strong relationships and open communication in place at HFA meant that supervisor and supervisee could use these moments of discord productively—as a jumping-off point for learning more about how to make the relationship work.

Outcomes of Using Reflective Supervision

Campbell remembers, "A big challenge was being in an agency where outcomes were foremost. It's important to convince the administration that *not* telling people what to do will lead to better outcomes. It's a huge leap of faith on their part."

HFA experienced a dramatic increase in positive outcomes after implementing reflective supervision with an emphasis on strengths-based relationships and mutual competence. Home visiting rates went up from less than 70% each month to routinely more than 80% (Bernstein et al., 2001). Developmental screening completion rates increased from 50% to more than 85% during the 18-month transition period, and both rates have remained at these higher levels for the last 12 months (Bernstein et al., 2001). These positive outcomes provide powerful evidence that investing time in providing supervision does not decrease staff productivity but, rather, quite the opposite: It increases staff effectiveness on the job.

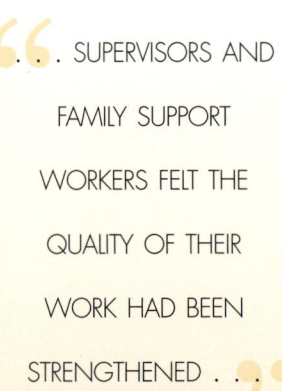

". . . SUPERVISORS AND FAMILY SUPPORT WORKERS FELT THE QUALITY OF THEIR WORK HAD BEEN STRENGTHENED . . ."

PHOTO: MARILYN NOLT

In addition, a recent survey of staff found that both supervisors and family support workers felt the quality of their work had been strengthened as a result of the change. Staff members, in particular, saw themselves as being more effective in their role of helping parents understand their children's development, and all felt that the quality of supervision had improved dramatically from the beginning of the project (Bernstein et al., 2001).

Even with such powerful outcomes, resisting the temptation to solve problems and prescribe solutions is difficult to do at times. Campbell notes:

> Reflective supervision is not a natural thing to do without support. Victor Bernstein calls it "forces of risk"—the daily responsibilities that push you away from reflection. It's easy to slide away. At the same time, people feel more competent with reflective supervision, and you see the positive outcomes of people using reflective supervision who feel confident in their work. But it is very hard to stick with. When any of us are under pressure, and this work is hard, we default to telling someone what to do. And it's not that it's wrong [to do that]. It just isn't as effective. The forces of risk are pretty powerful.

CONCLUSION

Although they struggle at times with the stresses of the work and the challenges posed by the families they serve, staff members are committed to maintaining the organization's focus on reflection, collaboration, and mutual respect. By providing both supervisors and family support workers with support through supervision as well as with new approaches to use in the work, Healthy Families has found that reflective practice is an important way to encourage continuous learning among staff members and to enhance services to families. This philosophy is best expressed by supervisor Charlene Giles who observes, "Reflective supervision is not something you learn to do and then you're done. It's a continuous process—you never stop learning, but you revisit the concepts and refresh them once in a while."

SUGGESTED ACTIVITY

Developing staff and supervisors' observation skills was a major thrust of Healthy Families' training efforts, and both groups continue to use observation as a primary method of gathering information. To learn more about your own approach to supervision and staff development, this activity suggests inviting a colleague, mentor or supervisor to

QUESTIONS TO THINK ABOUT

1 Think of a recent issue that a staff member was struggling with. In what ways did you or could you:
- get more information about the issue?
- help the staff member rely on his or her observation skills?
- help the staff member evaluate appropriate responses?

2 Healthy Families made a commitment to a strengths-based approach in which organizational, staff, and family strengths are used as a foundation for continuous learning and skill development. Consider the following questions as you reflect on your organization and your experience as a leader.
- What are your strengths as a program leader?
- What are your program's strong points?
- How might these strengths serve as a foundation for encouraging a reflective, strengths-based approach?

3 Healthy Families experienced strong positive outcomes as a result of using reflective supervision, outcomes that helped them quantify this tool's effect on the program, on staff, and on families. As you think about outcomes, consider the following questions:
- What do you think are or might be the most accurate measures of your program's effectiveness?
- Does your program track these measures? If not, how could you begin tracking them?

observe your interactions with a supervisee. You can approach this activity in several ways:
- With your staff member's permission, ask a supervisor, mentor, or colleague to observe a supervisory session.
- With your staff member's permission, tape record or videotape a supervisory session with him or her.
- Take careful notes during a supervisory session with your staff member (you may want to explain ahead of time what you are doing).

Afterward, debrief with your observer or take a few moments on your own to reflect.

If you are new to reflective supervision, think about the following questions:
- What worked well in this interaction? What didn't seem to work so well?
- What moments in the conversation felt comfortable or awkward? Why might that be?
- What did you learn about (or from) your staff member in this conversation?
- If you could redo this conversation, what would you like to do differently?

If you are more experienced with reflective supervision or wish to consider additional questions, think about the following:

- What feelings did you notice in yourself during the conversation?
- Did you experience any particularly strong (positive or negative) reactions during this meeting?
  What might have been the cause?
- Did your staff member seem to experience any particularly strong (positive or negative) reactions
  during this meeting? What might have been the cause?
- Was your body giving you any cues (e.g., beating heart, sweating, damp palms) during the conversation? If so, what might have been the cause?
- In reviewing the session, how would you describe your relationship with this staff member? How do you think this relationship supports his or her functioning on the job?

With your staff member, discuss your experiences of the session. What inferences did you make about his or her experience of the supervisory discussion? Were these accurate? Did he or she have a different experience from your own? In what ways?

How It May Look in Practice: Individual Supervision Session

During one-on-one supervisory sessions, supervisors at Healthy Families use thoughtful inquiry and observations to support staff in formulating individualized responses to families' needs. The vignette below provides an example of how this kind of interaction might look in a family support program.

Corey, who has 3 years' experience, is a family support worker and home visitor. She requested a meeting with her supervisor, Geoff, to discuss working with Shannon, mother of 1-year-old Tyler. Shannon has missed her last four appointments with Corey.

G: *How are things going? I know the last time we talked you were leaving for a long weekend at your parents' house. How was that?*

C: *It was really nice to get away, and it's always good to see them. It was just what I needed. Work has been a little stressful lately.*

G: *What's going on?*

C: *Well, you know Shannon? She missed another one of our visits. That's the fourth one. I don't know what to make of these no-shows. When I call to follow up, she always wants to reschedule. We set another date and time, I call to remind her, and she says, "Yes, yes, I remember." Then I get there and nobody's home.*

G: *How does that feel for you?*

PHOTO: MARILYN NOLT

C: *It makes me so— [pause] well, it's frustrating. I hate getting there and find I've wasted a trip. And, quite honestly, I feel like I'm getting the runaround. I'm not sure Shannon is really open to services right now. I wonder whether other families might benefit more from our time.*

G: *Those are both valid questions. And it sounds like this family has been a challenge. But before we talk about what to do, maybe you can tell me what your experiences with Shannon and Tyler have been besides the no-shows?*

C: *Well, I've been working with them for 8 months, but the last time I saw them was in December [4 months prior] because Shannon's missed every appointment since then.*

G: What happened at that last visit?

C: Well, it was my second visit with the family. Their living situation struck me as pretty chaotic. They live with what seems to be a mixture of friends and relatives, and the people living there seem to change fairly often. The house was messy, but that didn't bother me as much as the kitchen. It wasn't just messy, it was really dirty—one of the worst I've seen. That set off alarm bells for me since Shannon was referred to us from Social Services for possible neglect.

G: Did anything else about that visit concern you?

C: Shannon's personal hygiene wasn't so good, and neither was Tyler's. And Tyler was wearing shorts, no shirt, and no socks—even though it was freezing that day and the house was pretty cold. As it turned out, they had their heat turned off. So we spent most of that visit figuring out what to do to get the heat going again.

G: Do you know anything about Shannon's history?

C: Not a whole bunch. I do know that Tyler's dad is no longer in the picture. Apparently, he left as soon as Shannon got pregnant. She thinks he's gone to live with family in Missouri. Shannon's mom died when she was 10. She was raised by an aunt who—and I'm reading between the lines here— wasn't much interested in her. She didn't know her dad. As far as Tyler goes, her pregnancy went pretty smoothly. They were referred because Child Protective Services thinks Shannon needs help with her parenting skills.

G: How do you think all of this feels from Shannon's perspective?

C: To be fair, she's got a lot on her plate right now. The last time I talked to her, she was just about to start the Welfare to Work program. And Tyler doesn't have what you'd call an easy temperament— he struck me as a pretty demanding baby.

G: How do you think Shannon felt about being referred to us?

C: Well, it wasn't her idea, that's for sure. Basically, Social Services told her she had to participate in the program. So there was that dynamic there as well. But, you know, I really felt like in the second visit we were starting to click.

G: Based on what you know about her, how do you think Shannon feels about relationships?

C: [long pause] Well, she hasn't had such great experiences with them. I got the impression she basically raised herself after her mother died. And Tyler's dad doesn't sound exactly like Prince Charming. He wasn't supportive during the pregnancy and now isn't in contact with them at all.

G: I'm wondering whether Shannon's interactions with you are a reflection of what she needs to do to survive: protect herself. A lot of the parents we work with take a long time to trust us, whether it's because of their past experiences with relationships or just the fact that they might see us as one more bureaucrat out to make their lives harder.

C: Like maybe she's testing me? Will I really be there for her? Will I really keep trying?

G: Yeah, maybe it's something like that. What do you think?

C: I hadn't thought of that. It would make a lot of sense. Maybe that's why she keeps rescheduling. She wants to see if I'll come or if I'll abandon her.

G: Exactly. Maybe this testing is how Shannon is learning to trust you or learning that you're trustworthy. At least it's one hypothesis to explain what you've been experiencing. But you started our discussion off today with two important questions: Is Shannon open to services and, given her no-shows, would another family benefit more from the program? I want to get back those. What do you think?

C: Well, given our talk today, I'm not sure how I feel. I think we should at least give it a little more time, [pause] although to be honest, I still feel kind of frustrated. But at least now I can put myself in Shannon's shoes. How about if I try again to connect? I'll call to set up a time, but maybe I'll also write Shannon a note, letting her know how much I'm looking forward to seeing them and that I've been thinking of them lately and wanted to catch up. Then, let's say if she's a no-show for three more visits, you and I talk again about whether to keep them in the program.

G: That sounds fair. Let me know how your next call—and hopefully your next visit—goes. This family is pretty lucky to be working with you.

by Rebecca Parlakian and Trudi Norman-Murch
Southwest Human Development Interviewees:
Ginger Mach-Ward, Executive Director
Trudi Norman-Murch, Director of Services for Children with Disabilities Department
Sue Felchle, Early Intervention Program Manager
Kelli Hansen, Early Intervention Home Visitor

Southwest Human Development
Where: Phoenix (Maricopa County), Arizona
Mission: To provide a continuum of quality services for children and families that respect diversity and foster self-sufficiency by supporting parents as the primary educators of their children
Target Population: Young children and their families who face challenges related to health, child abuse and neglect, mental health, poverty, and disabilities
Program Model: Community-based service provider
Introduced Reflective Supervision: 1993
Catalyst for Change: Participation in ZERO TO THREE's CityTOTS seminar, a program designed to improve the training available for infant-family practitioners
Frequency of Supervision: 2 hours per week for supervisors, direct-service staff, and administrative staff; supervision includes both individual and group meetings

Background on Southwest Human Development
Southwest Human Development was founded in 1981 by Ginger Mach-Ward to provide services to children with disabilities and their families. In 1982, the agency was made a Head Start grantee. Since then, Southwest has continued expanding, adding to its range of services a training and technical assistance project, child protective services work, a program for infants and toddlers with disabilities, a neonatal intensive care unit follow-up program, and an infant mental health program.

This case study focuses on the implementation of reflective supervision and relationship-based approaches in one department within Southwest Human Development, the Services for Children with Disabilities (SCD) Department. The change effort described here also occurred to a large extent in other departments and programs at Southwest.

PHOTO: MARILYN NOLT

IMPLEMENTING REFLECTIVE SUPERVISION

Staff within the Services for Children with Disabilities (SCD) Department, the focus of this case study, provide Part C Early Intervention, assistive technology, and Head Start Disabilities services to children and families in the Greater Phoenix area. The department has a staff of 85, including early interventionists, occupational therapists, physical therapists, speech and language pathologists, early childhood special educators and assistive technology specialists.

Prior to 1992, "agency programs, for the most part, operated autonomously. People were very independent, very capable, and accustomed to doing the work on their own," remembers Executive Director Ginger Mach-Ward. Supervision was limited, and generally focused on administrative issues (billing, caseloads, and grant writing) or handling crises. Trudi Norman-Murch, director of the SCD Department, describes intervention services at that time as being primarily child- and disability-focused, with relatively less explicit attention paid to promoting parent-child relationships or children's social-emotional development. Many of the services were clinic- or center-based.

To assist with the transition to reflective supervision, Southwest engaged consultant Judith Bertacchi, now of the Ounce of Prevention Fund, to assist with the transition. As the concepts of relationship-based work and reflective supervision were introduced

within the SCD Department and throughout the agency, a number of concrete changes took place. Among the most notable are those discussed in the following sections.

REGULAR SUPERVISION AND TEAM MEETINGS

Before 1992, supervisory structures at Southwest tended to be rather unclear and meeting times, irregular. Now, as Trudi Norman-Murch says, "If you wake someone up in the middle of the night and ask, 'Who is your supervisor?' they should know the answer!" All SCD employees, both direct-service and administrative staff, receive approximately 2 hours of supervision per week on a consistent basis. This supervision includes individual, small group, and team meeting sessions. Supervisor Sue Felchle notes, "I look at my calendar and know that I will see everyone on my team at least once a week in different contexts." This frequency of interaction is a significant increase in regular, planned contact.

The content of individual supervision and team meetings also changed with the introduction of reflective supervision. Before, "team meetings were spent on organizational and structural matters," Felchle says, but "the purpose [now] … is to share the work and our experiences with families." Meetings, she says, "help draw us together." This collegial support is crucial in the human services field where the issues addressed by staff are often complex, emotionally charged, and intensely stressful.

JOB DESCRIPTIONS AND PERFORMANCE REVIEWS

Job descriptions, the hiring process, and performance reviews all have changed as a result of the shift to relationship-based work. Previously, the emphasis was on technical, disabilities-related skills and on administrative responsibilities. Jobs are now defined around a cluster of key relationship-based skills that are standard across the organization. Position-specific skills are added to complete the description. Two excerpts from an SCD job description, shown in Examples 1 and 2, illustrate how relationship-based principles have been integrated into staff members' performance expectations.

Example 1: Job description excerpt from Southwest Human Development

Implements early intervention services as described through the collaborative planning process (Individual Education Plan or Individual Family Service Plan)

- Practice reflects understanding of the centrality of relationships in supporting children's and family's growth and development. Is able to establish a therapeutic alliance with teachers/families on behalf of identified child.
- Integrates intervention services into ongoing home or classroom routines in a developmentally appropriate manner.
- Facilitates collaboration with parents, teachers, and other professional staff through regular contact, paperwork, and designated team meetings.
- Provides intervention services with frequency specified in the I.E.P. or I.F.S.P.

Example 2: Job description excerpt from Southwest Human Development

Uses supervision effectively, takes initiative to secure professional development opportunities, and applies relevant information in the work setting.

- Actively participates in supervision that is regular, reflective, and collaborative in nature. As appropriate, takes the initiative to seek supervisory support.
- Is able to accurately identify areas of mastery and areas targeted for growth and development. Seeks assistance and guidance when needed.
- Incorporates constructive direction from supervisor to improve job performance.
- Accepts responsibility for the quality of job performance and makes changes as needed.
- Maintains awareness of current professional information in the fields of activity, undertakes regular and ongoing efforts to maintain competencies in the skills used, and incorporates and demonstrates new knowledge and skills on the job.

The agency also examined its system of performance reviews, which previously had little consistency across the organization. The evaluation process was redesigned to support the organization's shift to relationship-based work. Norman-Murch observes, "Our approach to performance reviews helps us focus on relationship skills; the kind of relationships that we have with families, the way we are with our colleagues, the way we're able to reflect on ourselves is part of our job." For example, during a recent performance review, a therapist in the Early Intervention program discussed her difficulties making the shift from spending all her time working directly with the children on her caseload to learning effective ways of sharing her expertise with team and family members.

In the past, the performance review tended to be a stand-alone event. Now it is understood to be part of an ongoing conversation. Felchle notes, "We have one rule: No surprises. We will never bring up a problem or concern for the first time during a performance review. We are committed to talking about issues as they arise during the course of the year."

Staff members are asked to reflect on the successes they have experienced in the previous year and to identify goals for the coming twelve months. The review is the product of the staff member's self-assessment, the supervisor's observations, and their joint discussion. Norman-Murch elaborates: "We have the opportunity to talk about the issues which are most problematic. If you have a staff member who does good work but who has poor communication skills, you might be tempted to let it slide. Now we have a framework and multiple opportunities to discuss the tough stuff. As a supervisor, that's where the bravery is."

> " NOW, THE REVIEW PROCESS FORMS A PARTNERSHIP [BETWEEN SUPERVISOR AND SUPERVISEE] IN WHICH BOTH OF YOU MAKE A COMMITMENT TO WORK ON YOUR GOALS TOGETHER. "

The *feeling* associated with performance reviews has also changed. Felchle says, "I remember being an early interventionist. We had an opportunity to go in once a year and talk about our job. Now, the review process forms a partnership [between supervisor and supervisee] in which both of you make a commitment to work on your goals together. We know we will have many more chances to keep on talking about them." Norman-Murch notes that this change in the staff's perception of supervision was an important achievement for the program: "That feeling of somebody being there with you is the most important and hardest to achieve. The wariness [people feel around] an authority figure is very hard to counter." Southwest believes that its commitment to involve as many staff members as possible from the beginning was key to securing their support and acceptance of the change.

SERVICE DELIVERY MODELS

SCD staff members noted that their approach to service delivery, to some degree, evolved from their understanding of relationship-based work and reflective practice. Most profoundly, staff came to understand that their primary job was to establish a therapeutic alliance with families on behalf of the child rather than provide direct treatment to the child. This practice involved helping family members understand how they could contribute to and support their child's treatment services. Staff members also realized that providing services in the "natural environment" referred to more than the physical location of the intervention. Rather, they came to understand it as the child's context of family relationships, rituals, and routines.

PHOTO: MARILYN NOLT

TOOLS TO SUPPORT REFLECTIVE SUPERVISION

"It's not so easy to 'be reflective,' especially when there is very little in your professional training that prepares you to be," says Norman-Murch. She explains that, both within the agency as a whole and within the Disabilities Department, staff members utilized specific tools and strategies to support reflective practice and relationship-based work. The following sectiosn describe some that have been the most useful.

Hiring a Mental Health Consultant

The Early Intervention team added a mental health specialist to the staff who has become increasingly involved in all aspects of the program. Her role is to

- assist staff in understanding the needs of families; help them identify ways in which their own beliefs, values, and attitudes may be affecting their ability to form a partnership with families; and
- identify times when referral for outside mental health consultation might be appropriate.

Although, at first, the mental health specialist was included only in more extreme or crisis situations, she is now a part of all team meetings and discussions.

The SCD management team also contracted with a psychologist from Arizona State University to facilitate a monthly management meeting devoted to addressing difficult supervisory issues. Incorporating outside supervision from a mental health professional added an important new dimension to the program's work.

Training in Strengths-Based Approaches

Staff members from the Disabilities Department reported that training provided by The Portage Project, of Portage, Wisconsin, was valuable in helping them learn how to put into practice a strengths-based approach. Skills introduced in these sessions included ways of

- using "partnering language" with families;
- turning judgments into questions; and
- taking a functional approach to identified capacities and resources (e.g., How can this strength be used as a support or foundation?)

Norman-Murch summarizes, "We're learning techniques to slow ourselves down and not jump to conclusions." Felchle agrees: "We are realizing that doing something *right now* might not be the best intervention." Clearly, a staff member's ability to pause and gather more information before reacting also spotlights an important parallel for families.

Observation and Videotaping

Supervisors regularly join staff members on home visits as a way to provide a common base of experience for discussion and reflection. Although, at first, this co-visiting was uncomfortable for some, it has become a routine part of the program. Supervisors typically join in on the home visits, for example, getting down on the floor to interact with the child and participating in conversations with the parent and staff member.

When new staff members are introduced to reflective supervision, they are told that co-visits are a standard part of the program. Thus, no one feels singled out when they occur. Supervisors offer to accompany home visitors on any visits—those that are especially stressful or those that are positive—and initially, supervisors give staff a choice as to which visits they attend. Feedback is strengths-based and reflective in nature.

The Disabilities Department along with the agency as a whole has also begun to use videotape to support reflective work. Staff received training on using videotape interventions to support positive parent-child interactions and to enhance team problem solving. Follow-up in individual supervision and team meetings has helped to encourage staff members in their efforts to learn this new strategy.

Challenges to Implementing Reflective Supervision

As with any organizational change, challenges did come up during the implementation of reflective supervision. Some staff members resisted the increase in meetings and the increased time spent on supervision and peer mentoring. "We moved from a system where people were quite autonomous," Felchle remembers. When the idea was first introduced, she adds, "you felt like you didn't know why [leadership] had this interest in changing." This reaction shifted as time went on. She continues, noting that "regular contact has become more welcome and feels more like help. Teams realize how much peer support they get [in meetings]."

For managers, introducing reflective supervision sometimes meant being on the receiving end of negative feedback and intense emotion. Norman-Murch remembers, "So many times I felt that my intent was misunderstood and I was blindsided by hostile reactions." An effective coping strategy proved to be applying the concepts of reflection internally: "I had to get more reflective and self-aware myself. I don't personalize [those reactions] as much as I used to."

The whole process took time—considerably longer than management or the staff had anticipated. Ginger Mach-Ward and Trudi Norman-Murch credit their consultant, Judith Bertacchi, with supporting them and the agency through the 5-year transition. "She helped us prioritize our needs and pace ourselves." (Norman-Murch & Ward, 1999, p.12).

OUTCOMES OF USING REFLECTIVE SUPERVISION

At a fundamental level, staff members now see the work they do in a different way. Supervisor Felchle observes:

> People aren't as judgmental of parents anymore. Instead they wonder what's going on. [Reflective supervision has helped us] broaden our view of what the work is. We look at the whole family—their relationships with each other, with the neighbors, with the community. Our main purpose is to support the development of the child, but the child's experience in the family makes a difference [in every facet] of his [or her] life.

This new level of family-centeredness, a by-product of training on reflection and observation, has resulted in more individualized services to families.

Staff members understand that the way they interact with families and colleagues will greatly influence the effectiveness of their work. They have also come to see their professional specialty (e.g., speech therapy) as a tool to support positive caregiver-child relationships, which then support children's learning and development. As a result, families have a much higher level of participation in intervention services than before. (This increased participation may not always happen easily. Kelli Hansen notes, "Some families still say, 'There's my child. I'll be in the other room.' It's trial and error, and takes extra effort with some families.")

CONCLUSION

In this fast-growing agency, reflective supervision has provided consistency—a clarity about "who we are as an organization," says Executive Director Ginger Mach-Ward. At an operational level, the most profound change brought about by reflective practice is at the same time both simple and complex. Notes Felchle, "It means that you are in it together, that nobody has to do it alone. During a change, or when you are doing something really scary, you've got support. Families [too] don't have to face things alone." Far from being disconnected from program goals, relationship-based work has enhanced and enriched Southwest's already-strong belief in the importance of strengths-based, family-centered services.

SUGGESTED ACTIVITY

Performance reviews at Southwest consist of a discussion of successes ("areas mastered") and a discussion of goals for the coming year ("areas to be worked on").

1 Brainstorm your own "areas mastered" and "areas to be worked on." Sit down with your supervisor or mentor to

QUESTIONS TO THINK ABOUT

1 Southwest focused a lot of attention on rethinking job descriptions to ensure they addressed the new skills and "way of being" that they were trying to achieve through the use of reflective supervision. The following questions can guide this process:

- In your opinion, what skills and qualities would describe an exemplary direct-service staff member?
- Review the job description for a direct service position at your organization. Do the skills and qualities you identified above match the job description used by the organization? If not, brainstorm what could be added or changed to align the two.
- What skills and qualities must staff members bring with them? Which of these skills and qualities can you teach or develop in others?

2 At Southwest, staff members began to see their professional specialty as a tool to support positive parent-child relationships, which then support children's learning and development. With this in mind, consider the following question.

- In your role as a program leader, how are you able to support positive supervisor-staff relationships? How do your efforts contribute to families' learning and development?

3 Trudi Norman-Murch remembers that one of the initial challenges of introducing reflective supervision was receiving negative feedback from staff members or feeling as though her "intent was misunderstood." In dealing with negative reactions, consider the following questions:

- Can you think of a time when you introduced a change or suggestion that garnered negative feedback from staff?
- How did you respond?
- Would you choose this response again? If not, why not?
- When we feel misunderstood, our tendency sometimes is to react immediately. Often, this tendency doesn't lead to the end we desire; as Sue Felchle observes, "doing something right now might not be the best intervention." What techniques do you use—or could you use—to avoid acting on these immediate impulses?

discuss professional development opportunities for the coming 6 months to 1 year.

❶ Sit down with one of your staff and invite him or her to do the same.

How It May Look in Practice: Staff Meeting

How It May Look in Practice: Staff Meeting

All SCD employees, both direct-service and administrative staff, receive approximately 2 hours of supervision per week, which includes a combination of individual, small group, and team meeting sessions. Each of these contexts is an important opportunity to support staff as they use a family-centered, collaborative approach in their work with families. The following vignette, set in an early intervention program, provides an example of how staff meetings might be used as an opportunity to practice reflective supervision.

Roberta, the site supervisor, is facilitating a staff meeting of early intervention professionals. One meeting per month is devoted to staff development. This week, Sherry (an occupational therapist who has recently graduated from a Master's program) will be discussing a family on her caseload. Her colleagues are invited to provide thoughts, guidance, and feedback. Note: The following vignette was adapted from Zeitlin and Williamson (1994). Reflective questions in the following vignette are adapted from Copa, Lucinski, Olsen, and Wollenburg (1999).

R: *(site supervisor): Hey everyone, today Sherry's going to talk with us about working with Amaya and her mom.*

S: *(occupational therapist): [standing] Well, today I could use some ideas on how to support Cici and Amaya's relationship and help them get to know each other's cues better. I'm also a little concerned about Cici's age. I'd like to talk about any special issues I should keep in mind with a teen mother. Let me start out by telling you a little about Amaya. She's 7 months old and was prenatally exposed to cocaine. Amaya has some developmental delays but seems to have the most trouble with regulating her emotional states. She'll do things like cry and cry for hours on end. Her mom, Cici, is 18 and a single mother. She's completed a drug rehab program, but she's still being monitored by Child Welfare to keep custody of Amaya.*

B: *(a colleague): What's their relationship like—Cici's and Amaya's?*

S: *Well, sometimes Cici is really affectionate and responsive, but at other times—mostly when Amaya is crying or spitting up—she gets really, really angry with her. Cici seems to see Amaya's behavior as being spoiled. Or manipulative, I guess.*

H: *(a colleague): Sherry, what does it feel like to work with this family?*

S: *Huh. I never thought about that. I guess I feel a little…well, powerless. It's like I think I know what the problem is, but nothing I try seems to really make a difference. It's hard to go on visits and never really see much improvement in their relationship. Honestly, it's kind of…depressing for me sometimes.*

T: *(a colleague): I know. I can relate to that, Sherry. I think we've all been there. One thing you might want to try is organizing interventions around daily activities—playing, feeding, bathing, you know. Help Cici take advantage of the everyday moments. Use those routines to show her how important she is to Amaya…show her all the good stuff she's already doing for her daughter.*

C: *(a colleague): I agree. I've found that using daily routines are a great way of building a stronger relationship between mom and child. I'd also suggest just asking questions. Like when Cici says that Amaya's spoiled, ask her things like "How do you think Amaya's feeling right now?," "What do you think she's crying about?," "How does it make you feel?" I'd also try to learn more about Mom's experiences and her history…, so you could ask things like "What was it like when you were growing up and you cried?"*

S: *[taking notes] These are all great ideas.*

R: *Sherry, what's working in this relationship? What are the family's strengths?*

S: *[pause] Well, Cici loves to sing, and one of the ways their relationship really works is when Cici is singing to Amaya. Silly songs, top 40, gospel—it doesn't matter. Amaya seems to love it, and her mom's singing is one of the few things that really helps her calm down when she's out of control.*

J: *(a colleague): That's interesting. It sounds like Cici has discovered at least one coping mechanism—singing—to help meet Amaya's needs when she's fussy.*

21

S: That's true. I hadn't really thought about it, but that's right. When I think about them each as individuals, I'd say that Cici's real strength is her personal determination. Here she is, 18 years old, and she's gotten herself through rehab and is making it as a single mom. She also has a great support system with her own family. Amaya's strong point is what I'd call her curiosity. She's a very alert baby, always looking around, taking the world in. Her mom says that Amaya was "born with her eyes wide open."

J: One of your questions was about Cici's age. In my work with teen moms, I've seen that, a lot of times, they need some extra support and nurturing. They're still growing up themselves, after all. But it can be tough to establish that kind of relationship. I've learned to be really observant…to take things at the mom's speed, when she's ready, so it doesn't seem like I'm some authority figure trying to tell her what to do.

S: You know, I think Cici might be feeling a little bit like that—even though I try really hard not to be prescriptive or tell her what to do. Hmm…I wonder if it would help if someone came with me on my next visit to give me another perspective?

R: I'm happy to go along, if you'd like.

N: (a colleague): Sherry, I'm wondering why you think Cici and Amaya have had some problems in their relationship?

S: Well, I think what's going on is that Cici is misinterpreting Amaya's cues. Like yesterday, the baby was crying hysterically when Cici was trying to dress her. From what I've seen of Amaya, she's very sensitive to touch—cool and hot, textures, you name it. I'd guess that dressing is probably really stressful for her. But Cici got so angry, saying that Amaya was "being disrespectful" and had a "nasty attitude." It just seems like they're getting their lines crossed and the messages aren't getting through.

C: When things like that happen, you can jump in and use your observations to help Cici begin to see Amaya's perspective. Try speaking in Amaya's voice and say something like, "Boy oh boy, Mom, I feel a little chilly. And that onesie itches me. I'm feeling a little scared right now." Sometimes doing that helps parents understand that their babies experience the world differently than they do.

S: That sounds like it could really work.

R: I think we've addressed some important issues today. Things like getting to know the parent's history, thinking about the family's strengths and what they bring to the relationship. All this information helps us identify the appropriate intervention. And strategies like using daily routines and speaking in the baby's voice are important tools to introduce new "ways of being" into the parent-child relationship. Are there any other ideas for Sherry before we break?

EVERY MODEL IS DIFFERENT:
IMPLEMENTING REFLECTIVE SUPERVISION

by Rebecca Parlakian and Cynthia Flauger
Early Intervention Services Interviewees:
Cynthia Flauger, Director
Barb Arndt, Teacher/Service Coordinator

Leaders of the programs profiled in this publication have made changes to organizational and supervisory practices, introducing more opportunities for staff reflection and continuous learning. Most frequently, these changes have included the introduction of regularly scheduled individual supervision, group supervision, or both. There are, however, many additional ways of providing staff members with support and opportunities to learn from the work. For example, the Early Intervention Services (EIS) program profiled below uses monthly staff meetings as an important way to promote ongoing learning, peer mentoring, and strengths-based, individualized services to families.

EIS has found that the structured use of staff meetings provides this organization with the best opportunity for all staff members to experience regular reflective supervision. The learning and support that occurs in these monthly meetings has helped to create a supportive, collaborative, and collegial environment at EIS, which supports the delivery of quality, relationship-based services to children and families. This program's experience offers an important perspective: Many roads can lead to reflective supervision.

In 1996, Early Intervention Services had the unique opportunity to participate in a reflective practice demonstration grant led by the Portage Project in Portage, Wisconsin. Through this grant, the Portage Project worked intensively with several infant-toddler programs to incorporate reflective supervision.

Through their work with Portage, EIS began implementing structured opportunities for staff support and learning. In addition to introducing monthly individual supervision, EIS staff members also began gathering for a monthly 3-hour meeting called mentoring time. (At EIS, *reflective practice* is referred to as "mentoring," and these terms will be used interchangeably within this profile.) Mentoring time is attended by all direct-service employees and by county staff who coordinate the program's

Early Intervention Services (EIS)
Where: Winnebago County, Wisconsin
Mission: To work in partnership with families of children ages birth to 3 years who have a significant developmental delay or disability. EIS provides programs and services (a) that will enhance the family's capacity to support their child's development within the context of the family and their community and (b) that are based on the strengths, needs, and priorities identified by the family.
History: EIS provides educational, therapeutic, and support services to children with disabilities, ages birth to 3 years, and their families. Established in 1992, EIS is a program within Goodwill Industries of North Central Wisconsin, Inc. The Winnebago County Department of Human Services contracts with Goodwill Industries (and, by extension, EIS) to provide early intervention services to its birth–3 population.
Target population: Children ages birth–3 years and their families
Introduced Reflective Supervision: 1996
Frequency of Supervision: On average, twice per month—one individual supervisory session and one group session (mentoring time)

services across Winnebago County. This peer mentoring and support session provides staff with a "committed time [in which] people can really think about who we are, why we do what we do, and why our work is so important," notes Teacher/Service Coordinator Barb Arndt, who is supervised by EIS Director Cindy Flauger.

Mentoring time begins with check-ins, which provide an opportunity for each staff member to share an experience, thought, or feeling related to either professional or personal issues in his or her life. The group then participates in a brief icebreaker exercise or team-building activity. Most of the meeting is spent discussing a specific case that focuses on work with a family in the program. Arndt explains, "We look at what [our colleague's] question is about the family, and [we gather more information] by asking what has worked, what they've tried, what the family's strengths are, and what the family has tried." The discussion format for these cases has, in many ways, become an organizing model for how staff members respond to challenging situations associated with the work. Director Cindy Flauger notes that the case discussion is useful because it asks staff to reflect "on the strengths of all the people involved and look at the whole picture before we try to fix it. We still want to jump to solutions sometimes and using [the case format] helps us manage that impulse."

EIS continues to convene monthly mentoring meetings, even after the conclusion of their planned work with Portage Project staff, because staff members value this learning opportunity. In fact, Arndt calls these meetings "sacred time." Because the grant also provided funding for staff participation in mentoring time and supervision, EIS had to make a conscious decision to maintain these supports as a core part of its program infrastructure when the grant monies were exhausted. This fiscal commitment has been made and supported by leadership within EIS as well as by its employer and contracting agency.

Over time, the use of mentoring shifted from being an interesting experiment at EIS to a necessary and natural part of how the program now operates. Notes Flauger,

> We are very fortunate that our contracting agency [the Winnebago County Department of Human Services] and our employer [Goodwill Industries] supports this use of our time and resources because it's not conventional. In fact, I think that other organizations sometimes look at activities like these as being more of an expense than an investment. After the grant funds wound down, we have still been able to provide this by absorbing the cost of staff time into our program operating budget. While we haven't done a cost/benefit analysis, it's only natural to conclude that direct-service staff will do a better job if they feel supported. The next leap is that children and families will be better supported as a result, and that's the ultimate goal of a reflective approach.

SUGGESTED ACTIVITY

At your next group meeting, ask a staff member to lead a case discussion about a family with whom he or she is working. To do this, use the guidelines suggested below:

1 Give your staff member plenty of notice to prepare. He or she should be ready to discuss the family's history, his or her relationship with the family, family members' strengths and vulnerabilities, his or her work with the family to date, and his or her questions about the family. Although the staff member will not necessarily be "presenting" on each of these issues, these topics may come up in the group discussion.

2 Allow your staff member to begin by highlighting
   • Issues or questions that he or she would like feedback on and assistance with from colleagues
   • The family's history and experiences with the program

3 Introduce the open-ended questions below (Copa et al., 1999) as one possible format for case discussions. Although these questions are not a "recipe," they provide some initial structure for the conversation and may be adapted to your program's needs and culture:
   • Tell the story (share facts, presenting issues, involvement, relevant personal experiences).
   • Acknowledge and clarify facts and feelings: "How does it feel to work with this family?"
   • Clarify the focus of the discussion: "What do you want the group to help you think about?"
   • Identify strengths and capacities: "What's working? How does it happen?"
   • Wonder about possible interpretations: "Why are things happening this way?"
   • Pinpoint areas for additional inquiry: "What do you need to know more about to understand this situation?" (Copa et al., 1999, p. 7)

4 At the conclusion of the discussion, summarize the main learning points and themes that were presented.

5 Solicit feedback from staff members about what they learned, liked, and disliked about the experience.

QUESTIONS TO THINK ABOUT

1 As you consider the previous profiles and the way that organizations use reflective supervision during staff meetings, think about the following questions:
   • In what ways do group meetings (e.g., staff meetings) support staff learning in your organization?
   • What are three activities for upcoming staff or team meetings that could enhance skill development and encourage peer support opportunities?

Makayla is a supervisor at an early intervention program. She is beginning today's staff meeting with check-ins.

M: Thanks for coming today. I know it's been a busy week. I wanted to start today's meeting off with check-ins, so we can get a sense of how things are going for everyone. I'll start. [pause] Well, I guess the week started off on a bad note. My husband got food poisoning. That's why I wasn't here on Monday and Tuesday. But things are looking up, and he's feeling much better.

C: M., that's awful. So glad to hear that Dan is doing better. [pause] Well, I'll go next. I had a great visit with the DeByrons—that new family on my caseload. They are really excited about working with us. I mean, pinch me, I must be dreaming!

S: That's really great. Things at work have been pretty calm for me this week, but at home, it's been nuts! My son's science fair project was due yesterday so we've been spending every night up to our elbows in paint and glue. But it was worth it. He was so proud of the finished product.

J: S., you'll have to bring in a picture. [pause, then throwing up her hands] Oh, my week has just been awful. One of my families was reported to Child Protective Services for neglect so I've been dealing with that. And then another one of my families moved away and I have no idea where. It's just been one frustration after another.

T: J., I think you get the prize this week. My families—knock wood—seem to be doing fine, although I'm drowning in paperwork. We have those reports due on Friday and, as usual, I've put them off until the very last minute. Talk about stress!

M: T., let us know if we can do anything to help. [pause] Thanks, everyone. I know it really helps me to hear where each of you is coming from. I'll try—I know we'll all try—to keep what you've shared in mind during our discussion today. It's good to know that we can turn to each another for support during the tough times and to celebrate the good stuff, too. If there's anything you'd like to discuss in more depth with me outside the meeting, feel free to drop by or give me a call. For today's meeting, I was hoping to talk with you about the new approach to home visits that the agency has proposed. I'd love to get your feedback on the information about this approach that Joyce circulated last week.

CONCLUSION

Organizations profiled in the previous case studies have found reflective supervision to be a crucial component in their efforts to provide quality services to children and families. Following are five key lessons learned from these programs:

1 *Positive changes in the relationship between parents and children often begin with positive changes in the relationship between supervisors and the staff.* When the supervisory relationship is open, supportive, and nonjudgmental, staff members are better prepared to meet the complex needs of the children and families in their care.

2 *Conflict during periods of change effort is inevitable.* Program leaders, even when they make every effort to be inclusive, open, and collaborative, must be prepared for some challenging moments when they are carrying out a change such as reflective supervision. Providing opportunities for calm discussions of differing opinions and conflicting feelings is helpful. Also helpful is regular supervision for supervisors to support them as they manage and respond to staff members' feelings and reactions to the change.

3 *Implementing reflective supervision is just one piece of a larger quality enhancement effort.* The process of introducing reflective supervision required concomitant changes in recruitment, training, curriculum, communication style, and performance assessment.

4 *Reflective supervision is more a way of being than a way of doing.* Reflective practice focuses on the development of positive, affirming relationships between supervisors and staff members, staff members and families, and parents and children. Within these relationships is where learning and change can take place.

5 *The emotionally intense nature of infant-family work poses special challenges for staff members—*

ST. JOSEPH'S COLLEGE CALLAHAN LIBRARY

3 1960 02391 854

and demands supportive, regular supervision. Acknowledging challenges, concerns, and ambiguities in the work is a crucial first step to helping staff members manage their own frustration and experiences with burnout. Reflective supervision also provides a framework for devising coping mechanisms that can help staff members manage the complex feelings and reactions that arise in their work with children and families.

❻ *Reflective supervision is not an all-or-nothing proposition.* Organizations can implement components of reflective supervision (including reflection, collaboration, and regular meetings) into their programs on an incremental basis.

Choosing to implement a major organizational change such as using reflective supervision is not the decision of one but of many. The programs profiled in the previous case studies represent countless voices joined together to effect a lasting and transformative change. Their experiences and outcomes provide a glimpse of what reflective practice may offer your program and its stakeholders—supervisors, staff members, and families alike.

APPENDIX 1: SUGGESTIONS FOR TRAINERS AND FACILITATORS

Trainers and facilitators who plan to use the case studies presented in this publication for group training purposes may wish to focus on a few of the primary themes introduced by the profiled organizations. These themes and suggested discussion questions are presented in the following table.

Theme	Suggested Discussion Questions
Reflection as a professional skill	• Would incorporating reflective supervision be useful to your program? Why or why not? • What does the use of reflective supervision offer a program? • Would using reflective supervision in your organization make a difference in the way the work is done? How?
Importance of thoughtful change management strategies	• Do you see any barriers to implementing reflective supervision in your program? How could they be addressed? • In your experience and based on what you've read, what are the key elements of a successful change effort? • Think about a recent (or upcoming) large-scale organizational change. What are several concrete ways you did (or can) involve staff members and solicit their input?
Enhancing and supporting the needs and culture of the program through reflective supervision	• What is one thing that really struck you while reading these case studies? Why? • What is one idea you'd like to try in your program? • How is your program similar to or different from some of the organizations profiled here? (perhaps appropriate for journaling or small group work)
Individual questions for reflection	• Which profile is most similar to my program? • Do I see myself providing reflective supervision? Why or why not? • Do I see reflective supervision being used in my program? Why or why not? • What aspects of reflective supervision might come naturally to me? • What aspects would I find difficult? • Where might I go for help in making changes in my work?

Trainers may also refer to the discussion questions at the conclusion of each c
training ideas and exercises.

This publication may be used on its own as a training or self-teaching tool or in co
for Program Excellence resources that focus on the important role of reflection a
ly programs. Both Look, Listen, Learn: Reflective Supervision and Relationship-Base
Questions: Building Quality Relationships with Families contain exercises that traine
in exploring these issues. To order these publications, please contact ZERO TO TH
department at 800-899-4301, or visit the ZERO TO THREE on-line bookstore at